I am
in Love
with my
LOCS!

AuthorHouse™ UK
1663 Liberty Drive
Bloomington, IN 47403 USA
www.authorhouse.co.uk
UK TFN: 0800 0148641 (Toll Free inside the UK)
UK Local: 02036 956322 (+44 20 3695 6322 from outside the UK)

Because of the dynamic nature of the Internet, any web addresses or links contained in this book may have changed since publication and may no longer be valid. The views expressed in this work are solely those of the author and do not necessarily reflect the views of the publisher, and the publisher hereby disclaims any responsibility for them.

Any people depicted in stock imagery provided by Getty Images are models, and such images are being used for illustrative purposes only.
Certain stock imagery © Getty Images.

This book is printed on acid-free paper.

ISBN: 978-1-6655-8577-4 (sc)
ISBN: 978-1-6655-8576-7 (e)

Print information available on the last page.

Published by AuthorHouse 03/01/2021

authorHOUSE

This book is dedicated to all those young girls
and boys who love and embrace their locs.
And to those who have yet to find the beauty in their hair,
may this book encourage you to embrace your uniqueness.

I have Afro-textured hair.

But my hair is different from Afro hair.

I used to be able to style my hair in an Afro.

But I decided I wanted my hair to be like my mum's.

You have to comb Afro hair, which I disliked.

But you do not have to comb my hair, which I love.

Some people like to touch my locs.

But I was taught to say, 'Please do not touch my hair.'

Some people think that only Afro hair can
be done in so many different styles.

But they are wrong!

My hair can be styled like this:

And this:

And even this:

There are lots and lots more styles that I could wear.

Can you think of any?

Some people think my hair is not 'normal' hair.

But what is 'normal' hair?

Everybody's hair is different.

But different is good!

Straight

Afro

Canerow

Twists

Locs

Braids

Curly

Embrace your uniqueness!

# About the Author

EJ Nembhard is a seven-year-old girl who loves to entertain. She has many aspirations, but the one that is constant, is becoming a model like her idol, Naomi Campbell. She also aspires to become a TV presenter, as is apparent through her YouTube channel.

EJ started her locs journey at the age of four and has never looked back. She enjoys standing out from the crowd, but feels that girls and boys with locs are somewhat underrepresented. EJ has an infectious personality. She loves the skin she is in and is super proud of the locs on her head.

To know EJ is to love EJ.

YouTube channel: Check in with EJ
Personal Instagram: @elahnijanae
Business Instagram: @locd.and.loaded.with
Etsy Store: LOCDandLOADEDwith
TikTok: @ejn2013
Illustrator's Instagram: @zaley_illustrations

Printed in the United States
By Bookmasters